GOP
DAMNED AMERICA

GOP
DAMNED AMERICA

D. A. Emert

To order additional copies of this book, contact:
Xlibris Corporation
1-888-795-4274
www.Xlibris.com
Orders@Xlibris.com

68706

America, we have well over a ten trillion national debt. Our economy is in the poorest condition since 1945. We are fighting wars in Iraq and Afghanistan.

So, where are we headed after eight years of G.O.P. president, G.W. Bush being the DECIDER making the BIG decisions??? A Russian professor is making a prediction that the United States will break up into four or six sections and that Alaska, which we purchased from Russia back in 1867 for about seven million, will go back to being a part of Russia.

Why would a professor from Russia think something like this could happen to America? Russia has been there done that. Russia in my younger years was the U.S.S.R or Soviet Union.

In the eighties, the Soviet Union, a super power, was having very bad economic problems, after fighting a nine year war in Afghanistan and trying to keep up with America in a cold war since 1945. The Soviet Union couldn't keep up. They went bankrupt, like Chapter 11; the super power had to down size.

The wall came down. East and West Germany became one country again. Many satellite countries that were part of the Soviet Union were allowed to rule themselves. The former U.S.S.R., a super power, went back to being called Russia by the rest of the world.

Russia was not the greatest place to live before the collapses of the Soviet Union, but it was much worse for years after. What happened in Russia is history.

History is a chance to learn from the past. If you saw someone try to beat a train at a rail road crossing and they lost, would you ever try it?? I think if you had any common sense at all you wouldn't. Our presidents have many advisors to give advice. It's sad but it seems none of the G.O.P. administrations, advisors under G.W. Bush, knew much about history. Maybe, if they did and had a little commons sense, our economy wouldn't have gotten hit by this train.

I caught the end of a GOP news sitcom saying history will look back on G.W. Bush and say he was a good president and helped our country. I've lived through 12 presidents, and I'm sorry but George W. Bush has got to be the worst.

If a history book were to ever say that G.W. Bush was a good president, the book would probably be published by a company owned by the same person who owns News Corp., Rupert Murdoch. He made a lot of money because of history. He saw what people were making money doing and he did the same. He got a lot of his ideas from what worked for Ted Turner.

Walter Cronkite and Mike Wallace, in my younger days, these were some of the news journalist I watched. They would tell me what was going on in America and the world. I got the who, what, when, where and why. After watching any news show, back then, I never thought I had to check the facts of any thing that they said. I remember asking my dad if we were democrats or republicans. He said democrats, we are not rich enough to be republicans, paused then added it doesn't really matter their all a bunch of liars.

Politics, unlike the news shows hasn't changed much since my younger days. I'm not a politician. I liked some of John McCain's ideas. I liked more of Obama's. Regardless, the G.O.P. has put our country in the crapper. They may be out of power, but they are still trying to flush. If both parties think being in power is more important than fixing our country, we are in big trouble.

If you see a politician or anybody on the media tell you to call your representative and tell them you want or don't want this or that, which is what you should do, you elect the politicians you can un-elect them. If you call your senator representative, make sure you know if what you're telling them to do or not to do is going to help you and not just help the person who wants you to call your representative.

Don't be mislead! G.W. Bush said many times. I lowered taxes, or I lowered your taxes. He did lower the taxes, but unless you are in the 4% or 5% of the top money earners, he didn't cut your taxes.

You're told if you take the Bush tax cuts away from this 5 %, small business will be hurt and they won't hire workers. What are you hearing on the news? Companies are laying off employees and our unemployment is the highest it's been in 45 years. The bush tax cuts were not stopped.

They didn't have bush's tax cuts during the Clinton years. During those years, we had low unemployment and small businesses did fine. How does a small business make money and grow to make more money? They sell a product or service to the average worker. The more the average worker has to spend means he can buy more from the small business.

The small business has to hire more help to keep up with the demand so he or she can make even more money. This puts another average worker buying more and creating demand from small business making more money and crating more jobs. This is simple common sense and its makes up more than 75 % of our economy.

If Bush would have gave the tax cuts to the 95% of the American workers and small business's making under $250,000 a year, instead of the 5% making over $250,000 wouldn't it have helped the 5% make more money, and create more jobs, making even more money for the top 5%. It could have even helped the top 5% grow to become the top 8% or higher. Many of small business creating 70% of the jobs do not make $250,000 a year.

The more the average worker gets to keep after deductions from his paycheck, the more they will spend helping business and our economy grow, common sense. The one thing I hear more and more from the GOP that makes no sense. A Flat tax. It is even pushed on the GOP news, business sitcoms. A Flat tax? The first time I heard this idea was on a GOP business sitcoms. Steve Forbes said it would help us by getting the rich to pay their taxes by stopping the tax loopholes they use to get out of paying taxes. The rich would still find a way to pay fewer taxes. But they would make less money because the average American would have to pay higher taxes giving them less to spend which would hurt our economy by giving them less to spend on small business.

The GOP changed the name of the flat tax; it's now called a fair tax.

The American worker lives week to week spending most of his pay, the same day he gets it. They pay bills, buy food; fill up the car with gas. Then at the end of the week, they have to borrow money form a friend for gas to get to work. Why should they pay the same tax rate as the person who doesn't bother or have to worry about the price of the fuel he's putting into his privet jet? It doesn't seem fair to me. Tell the GOP to call it what it is, an economy busting flat tax.

I heard Steve Forbes got his business from his father. It was left to him. This is a nice way to start a business. You start at the top. But most small businesses have to start at the bottom. If you're trying to start a small business it is easier to get started if you don't have to pay the same tax rate as Steve Forbes.

Mike Huckabee has a new show on the GOP news channel. He thinks a flat tax is a good thing so does Neil Cavuto. I have more on Steve, Mike and Neil. For now, I'll just say (the lights are on, but nobody is home.)

I have an idea for a fair tax that would put more money in the hands of the average American worker to put back into our economy. Lower taxes will help our economy. Putting more money in their hands to spend and get our economy going faster. Cut the social security tax in half. This could be done by taking the cap off. If you make under $200,000 a year this would give you more to spend helping small business grow. Social Security would still get the same or maybe more tax going in.

This would probably help 80% of the American workers. The GOP flat tax might help 10% for a year or two before our economy would be hurt by it.

I just heard Cheney say Obama should give tax cuts to those who can invest. That's what he and Bush did. Look where our economy is. The market is lower than its been in many years. Why? Fear. It seems like the GOP wants to get back in power. They think if the economy is still bad, you will help them get back in power, and forget they put us where we are. The GOP news did not want Obama to be president. The American people were smarter than that. Obama is our president.

The GOP news channel has business shows and started a business channel. Here are a few things I've heard on some of them and they never made O'Reilly's pin head list. I'll tell you why they made mine.

Gretchen Carlson, a former Miss America, is on the GOP and friends show. She is a college graduate and got very good grades but the GOP news never said in what. I would find it hard to believe it could be in journalism.

The Friday after Obama won the election, she said how the market had dropped since Obama had won on Tuesday. The DOW was down a few hundred points. The market has been dropping. Was it Obama's fault because he won? If this is the case how many thousands of points did the DOW drop since GOP said they were going to start the business channel?

Neil Cavuto is one of the top dogs on the business channel. He has a business sitcom on GOP news. He must have gone to business school. On his sitcom and other GOP sitcoms, they say if a business thinks its going to pay higher taxes it won't hire new workers.

I think if a business is selling more of a product or services then they have, they will hire more workers to make more money. The Fox business channel was started to make money. If they make more money they will pay more taxes. They hired a lot of people so they can pay more taxes.

Maybe if they had hired some people that went to business school, they may make it, and if not News Corp., will have a tax write off.

Another Cavuto. Talking about money going to the A.C.O.R.N. Cavuto said A.C.O.R.N. got a gold fish to vote. The pretty G.O.P. news contributor said, yes Neil and the gold fish probably voted for Obama.

Neil you should fire that girl, she thinks that gold fish is smarter than you.

More Cavuto on the economy. Neil said if someone bought a car it just goes off the lot, its not going anywhere.

I didn't go to business school so I asked my gold fish. It said the dealer would have the automaker bring another car to fill the spot on the lot. The automaker would hire a new worker, to build another car to replace the one the dealer got, to fill the spot on the lot. Neil that new worker might buy a car off that same lot.

Neil, I'm not attached to this gold fish if the GOP business channel needs it. I'll trade it for another car off that lot. It would be good for the economy.

Obama campaigned on lowering taxes for the middle class. The worker who would spend the extra take home pay and help our economy.

I heard the GOP news that 37% to 70% (depending on which sitcom) of American workers don't pay income taxes. This was on GOP news almost every day. Then in January they changed it.

The 37% to 70% still don't pay income tax, but they are paying payroll taxes.

So what is the payroll tax that they are paying? A payroll tax is income tax and other statutory deductions made by the employer from the employee's gross salary or wages. So you are not paying income tax, but you are paying payroll taxes which income tax is a big part of so what are they saying?

GOP news has a lot of lawyers on their sitcoms. They go to law school for years, they know how to talk to a jury, and they know how to bend the facts, misrepresent the truth to get their client off. Maybe, they could get a lot of the GOP news viewers to believe what their saying is fact. Maybe, they could get a good looking female lawyer, blond with great legs. I'd believe anything she said. That's right, they got one.

Maybe, they should send her over to the business channel. Give her Cavuto's job. She could save the GOP business channel ratings and have the channel buy the short skirts. Their news channel has been has been having their girls keep their legs crossed a lot tighter lately. She could say the same things Stuart Varney says and make them sound better. After Microsoft had a big layoff, Cavuto and the new senator from Illinois were talking about jobs created by the stimulus plan. Cavuto ask Senator Burris, Do you think a laid off Microsoft worker is going to take a job working on roads. Burris replied, maybe not but the person working on the road would be able to buy a new computer.

It's common sense, Burris knows that creating the stimulus jobs will help create more jobs in the private job market.

I could tell this wasn't the response, Cavuto expected, from Burris. He looked up eyes wide open, All he could say was good answer senator.

If a lawyer like Megan Kelly who plays a journalist on another GOP news sitcom had ask Burris the same question, as soon as Burris said, "maybe not but . . .", she would have broken in before he could explain how creating jobs creates more jobs, and said yes or no answer senator . . . . and not let him finish. She would talk over him and if he could be heard explaining how it would help the economy, she could object. People watching would have to strike what the senator said from their brain. We at the GOP news network don't want you to think the stimulus will work. We are going to go to commercial break. When we return, we'll ask Joe the plumber the same question. If we don't like his answer, we'll take another break and come back with a GOP news all star panel of people who are paid by us they will tell you what we want you to hear. This sounds stupid but it happens ever day on the 24 hour news channels.

The sitcoms that don't let someone explain or finish their answer are not news programs. They are big names and have cult like followers who think everything they say is fact. Really all they tell you is their opinion.

Jim jones was a cult leader many of his followers killed themselves because they believed what he said was fact. He was a nut case.

All the 24 hour news channels have sitcoms that should be taken as what they are . . . entertainment. Their opinion doesn't take it as fact. The bigger the nut the more people will watch. They create fear, and fear hurts the economy.

When the business sitcoms say stocks are not a good investment, many of their followers sell, hurting the economy. For years, while we were at war in Vietnam. gold went up by the end of the war. I believe it was over nine hundred dollars. After we got out of the war, it dropped back down to around three hundred dollars. The price of gold is back up over nine hundred dollars. The stock market is the lowest it's been in over forty years. What is the best thing to do for the economy and makes good business sense??? Buy low sell high.

Gold is high. The market is low.

Obama has only been president sixty days. The GOP has been complaining about how he is making our national debt higher than it's ever been. Let us look back in history. What did the last three GOP administrations do? They all added trillions to our national debt.

So, where were the complaints when these GOP presidents were making our debt higher? There was one administration that didn't raise our debt. Our economy was good. Businesses where hiring. Unemployment was low. Oh that's right, bill Clinton was president. He was not a conservative.

What is the GOP saying we should do? They say what would Ronald Reagan do? Reagan spent like there was no tomorrow. Well, tomorrow is here and it's not a nice day, unless you like unless you like a devalued dollar. Obama has to spend to create jobs and cut taxes on the average American who will spend the extra take home pay and help our economy. But we must get our national debt down. John McCain the GOP's choice for president said he would stop all aid to foreign countries. He said most of them don't like us anyway. This cost us billions every year. It should be stopped.

We call ourselves the most powerful nation in the world. McCain was going to cut our spending except the military spending. We have over a hundred military bases all over the world. It cost billions to keep them overseas. They help the economy in the countries they are located.

If we need this many military bases, put two in every state in America. This would put the spending in our country creating business and jobs in the private sector helping the economy.

The war with Germany was over in 1945. I saw the news around 25 years ago, Germans were protesting. They wanted us to get out of Germany. I was potty trained when we were at war in Korea. If we haven't got South Korea trained to defend themselves by now, good luck in Iraq. We have the technology to hit a dime on the other side of the world. We could still call ourselves a Super Power. We have to get our National debt down to nothing and get our economy going. We should cut the corporate tax to help small business, but the capital gains tax should remain the same.

A flat tax or a fair tax, as the GOP wants to call it, will kill our economy. It would give the average American less to spend hurting small business. The 5% tax cut in the stimulus will help but it's not enough. The GOP says 37% to 70% of us do not pay income taxes. So why not stop taking income taxes off the payroll checks of the lowest 40% to 50% of American workers. They will spend the extra take home pay and help the small business grow. The GOP should pass this with no complaints. Why would they? 37% to 70% of the lower incomes pay no income tax anyway?

When gas was going up, I was driving a PT Cruiser, it only had a 4 cylinder, but I was only getting around 22 MPG before gas was up to $3.00 a gallon. I bought a 91 GEO Metro, 3 cylinders for $200. I never got less than 40 MPG in this car. This was 90s technology. With a Multiport Fuel Injection or Electronic Fuel Injection, it would have had better MPG.

We will be using oil for many years to come and the price of gas is going up. It's 1.96 a gallon here on day 60 for Obama.

We all have to help get business going. Create jobs and get rid of our debt.

So how about a real fair tax. No nothing to do with the GOP flat tax. A fair tax that would create public and private jobs, build our infrastructure, helping our economy and our debt. It would let you do things and you would pay less. Add one dollar a gallon to the federal gas tax and a quarter to the state tax. I don't like to pay high gas prices, but think about it, you are probably paying more interest on your credit cards than what you would extra for gas. Get rid of your credit cards. It would give you more money to spend helping the economy. Your driving habits could put the gas demand down and the price would come down some, like it did when gas was over $4.00 a gallon. It's headed back up anyway.

For years, the politicians were getting most of their campaign money for their elections from big businesses and the very rich.

When you give someone money you expect something in return. You elect the politicians. If they do things you don't like, call, write, or email your representatives. Tell them what you think, but make sure it's what you want.

We should help business. I think we should cut corporate taxes, and keep capital gains taxes where they are.

We were the biggest industrial nation in the world, we became the biggest consumer nation. When our economy failed, the world followed by fixing our economy. We are helping the world economy. We can't just print more money; it just makes things cost more, by devaluing the dollar. We must create more jobs by building our infrastructure which will create more jobs and small business in the private sector. We must cut taxes on the lower American worker who will spend the extra money he takes home helping business grow and creating jobs. In turn, helping our economy.

We must get rid of our national debt. The sooner the better. Our National debt devalues our dollar which hurts the economy and the business.

Get rid of the Bush tax cuts for those making over $250,000 a year. You're not raising taxes, you are stopping a tax break to few rich people that helped make our national debt go up and hurt small business which hurts our economy. The Obama administration said they were going to stop the Bush tax cuts. The GOP and the GOP news channel are calling this raising your taxes. It would help lower our national debt. This tax cut for the top 5% didn't help our economy. It only helped the rich who didn't put the extra back into our economy. Have your representative stop it now.

We spent billions in aid to countries. Many of them don't even like us. John McCain said he would stop this. I think we should stop it. Many Americans need the same aid we give these countries. The GOP has our country close to bankruptcy. If we do hit bottom, we won't be able to help ourselves. Stop all aid to these countries. At least till we get rid of our debt. Have your representatives stop it.

We have over a hundred military bases in other countries. It cost billions to keep them there, and it would help our economy if these bases were in America. We don't need our military bases overseas. We would be just as powerful at a lot lower cost to the taxpayer. Call your representative to have our military in America.

During the first six years of the Bush Administration, the GOP news would call anybody who didn't agree with Bush, un-American. So if you watch fox news, it seems like they disagree with everything the new American president is trying to do to get our country out of the mess the GOP has gotten America into. So are you un-American if you allow yourself to be brainwashed by GOP news. They tell you things bloggers say on their shows. Some are just plan stupid. But fox thinks and many watching this show will believe it's true because it's on a news show which many believe to be fact.

Fox news called the AARP un-American because they were against the Bush plan to privatize social security. The AARP was right. Fox news and Bush were wrong. If social security was privatized it would have put hurting on many older Americans.

They would often say America, Love it or Leave it. I believe if our American nation is broken we should do what we can to fix it. Now, the GOP news is giving the people they have brainwashed a new nation, it's the fox nation. How un-American is this? But I guess this is one time they are being fair and balanced if your un-American and don't like our nation you can go to the fox nation.

That is something I didn't even think I would hear on the GOP news channel . . . . their own nation? I thought they got as low as they could with the Glen Beck show. But the sitcoms on fox can entertain in a funny way.

But this flat tax is not funny. They call it a fair tax, and it's not fair. It would hurt everybody, big business, and small businesses. I think it would even hurt Rupert Murdoch as much as it would the average American worker who wouldn't be able to have cable. We wouldn't have to worry about our economy. We wouldn't have one.

The economic stimulus was needed. Jobs create spending and spending helps small business grow creating more jobs.

The banks could not be allowed to fail. Their greed caused the housing bubble by getting high appraisals and passing loans that should never have been approved. The GOP news will tell you the banks were forced to make the loans and the people were forced to buy the houses. Anybody out there who was forced to buy a house, call me I have a brand new 2009 Studebaker I want you to buy.

We gave the banks billions. I thought this was a good idea. They would be able to make loans helping to create jobs and helping our economy. What do I hear? One bank getting stimulus money bought another bank. They are too big to fail. They should be made smaller.

Any carpenter, even Joe the plumber, will measure twice and cut once. Our government gave these banks billions to help our economy. They should know how it's going to be used. The GOP has been building our national debt since the eighties. This is what they called generational theft. Oh, that right, they only started calling it that since they are out of power. It was called Reaganomics, spend like there is no tomorrow. Well tomorrow is here, and it's not a nice day.

Clinton kept our national debt down and unemployment was low. Our economy was good. Then, along came Bush and it was back to reagonaomics. So where are we now?

We have to spend, but we have to get rid of the national debt that the GOP has made.

I believe this gas tax could get us going fast. It will help to create jobs. Thereby, helping the economy and ridding our Nation of this debt. I don't like high gas prices. Do you think a politician would try to pass a dollar a gallon federal gas tax and a quarter more state tax?

You are going to pay, you have to pay. If it's not a gas tax, it will be another tax and it will take longer. It took the GOP 25 years to put America in the crapper. We can get out; build a good infrastructure and economy while we get rid of our debt at the same time. Write, phone or email your representatives.

Unemployment would drop, the stock market would go up, and your dollar would buy more. Don't let them raise the tax a little now and a little later. Do it all at once. If it doesn't work, you can take it away. It will be a change you can see, and I bet you will think it is worth the two dollars a day it might cost at first.

You will have to demand it! CALL, WRITE OR EMAIL NOW!

Brit Hume, another GOPer on fox news said somebody's washing machine is going to break down and they will go out and buy a new one. Then, the economy will be better. People buying things will help the economy. But if somebody doesn't' have the money and the banks won't loan him the money, how will he buy his new washing machine? If the GOP fair tax ever gets through, the company making the washing machine will probably go out of business.

GOP news said 5% of Americans pay 50% of the taxes so a flat would lower taxes for 5% of Americans, raise taxes for 95% of Americans. So the GOP channel has to brainwash over half of Americans voters to get them to think paying higher taxes is good for them, and won't kill our economy.

Cavuto had three fox news contributors talking about unions. The last one to talk said we'd be better off if we got lower wages. If he was talking about Fox news contributors, he was right. If he was talking about the average American worker, he was wrong. Low wages would mean less to spend on small business which would be bad for the economy.

Because Obama is going to stop the Bush cuts for the rich. The GOP says he is raising taxes in a bad economy which will hurt our economy. Obama is not raising taxes. Bush only wanted his rich friends to have the tax cuts for ten years. Then, go back to what they were doing during in the Clinton years when our economy was great.

Fox news said if the rich think their taxes are going up, they won't hire. If a business is selling a product or service they will hire to sell more. They did it during the Clinton years when they were paying a higher tax rate and unemployment was low.

If your cable company has the fox business channel, call them and tell them to get rid of it, you don't need it, and the cable company has to charge you more to carry it. If they don't know the rich want richer and business's want more business. You can learn more about business on the history channel then the business channel.

So if you have the fox business channel call you cable company and demand they get rid of it.

An election add that ran a lot, had a guy saying, "I'm planning on hiring eight or ten more people next year, if Obama is elected, I'm not going to do it." This didn't make any sense to me. If hiring eight or ten people is going to make him more money, why wouldn't he hire them? He doesn't pay income taxes on the wages he pays them. He could get tax deductions on equipment. Business growth is tax deductable. Many small businesses don't make over quarter of a million a year.

I hear on the fox news if a business thinks it's going to pay higher taxes, they aren't going to hire. Let's use some common sense. If a small business is making a quarter of a million, they would hire new people if they could make a million a year. The small business knows this. The GOP knows this. The GOP doesn't want you to know this. This is politics. The GOP put us where we are. This is why they lost power. Now they want small government and to cut spending. They will cut spending if they make government smaller. Its just their idea of making government smaller is just pushing the cost of things onto the states. What does that mean to you? Higher state taxes, which are less you, have to spend. Hurts small business less jobs hurts economy.

The GOP wants to cut spending on everything except military spending. We can keep our million man army and still cut our military spending by trillions if we shut down at least 90% of our bases overseas. We don't need them. All the no bid jobs that Halliburton got from the Bush Cheney administration cost us. Cheney was the head of Halliburton before he was V.P. But I know the GOP wouldn't give them any bid contracts just because of Cheney, just like I know Cheney wouldn't drink beer and go hunting and shoot a man.

Free trade. Clinton did it and still thinks it's good. I think it was alright with Canada. I think it would be great to have free trade with Cuba. Oh that's right we don't talk to Cuba. We talk to Vietnam. John

McCain said we should not talk to Cuba. Did they do something worst than what Vietnam did?

Bush said we should have free trade because some countries are our friends. I'm sure Halliburton and Cheney are friends. Bush said we should have free trade because Americans want choices.

I think Americans want jobs and free trade would cause us to lose jobs to these countries. This can't help our economy. I just heard Obama fired the head of G.M. The auto makers are down sizing and laying off a lot of workers.

A lot of the small business that supply parts and services to the auto manufacturers are laying off or even going out of business. This cost America many manufacturing jobs. There are many things you can't buy even if you wanted to, made in America. They don't make them here anymore.

We should do more for our auto companies. The big banks broke the law making bad loans. Laws made because of the savings and loan problems years ago. When are we going to hear about some of the big bank CEO's going to jail? It would stop CEOs from letting greed get the best of them and stop this from happening in the future. Give them the same amount of time that Madoff gets; give him some one to talk to.

The market is going up now. I think too fast, but if you did get in, stay in, you'll make out. We do have to get our debt down, and I know no one would like a big gas tax hike now. If we don't do it soon, even China won't lend us money. The cost of everything is going up now. If we don't create jobs and get rid of our debt, it will get much higher. Tell your representative we need a much higher gas tax.

I have to go to the war and health care after a few more GOP ideas from Fox news that is on my pin head list.

The GOP news says higher taxes will hurt small business. The only way higher taxes will hurt small business would be if you had the Americans making under $200,000 a year paying higher taxes. They would not have as much money to spend at the small business. In turn, the small business would not be doing as much business so they would become even a smaller business.

So, now, the GOP news is telling you we need a fair tax where everyone pays the same tax. It would be a tax break for the rich and mean higher taxes for the lower and middle class. It would hurt all small business because the fair tax would be a sales tax on what you buy. Just think how much more you would have to pay for a car. This would hurt the auto companies costing even more jobs. All manufacturing companies would be hurt. The only people who would make out under a fair tax or flat tax would be the rich who make money off money how many jobs do these people create?

Rush Limbaugh, Bill O'reilly, Glenn Beck, Rupert Murdoch, and Sean Hannity will make out for a while until the sponsors can't afford them anymore because their business would be getting too small. Fox news is misleading the American public, they manipulate the facts to get the average American, to think something that is only good for the very rich, is good for them. Take Joe the plumber. He wanted to start his own plumbing business and wanted to make over a quarter a million a year. Who wouldn't want this? The fact is many small businesses don't make this after being in business for many years.

Obama's plan would have helped Joe and other small businesses grow and make more money. The GOP had to know this. But Joe is not too smart. He let McCain and the GOP use him. Here we have Joe an average American who wants to help us rich folks.

I think it's a good idea to share the wealth. You cut taxes for lower and middle class. Create jobs. They spend more; they are sharing their extra wealth with the rich. Helping their business grow, creating more jobs and wealth. The fair or flat tax would not let this happen. Joe should stay with what he knows, plumbing. He should stop trying to help the GOP, they have been hurting America for years with out his help.

Huckabee has his own show on the fox news channel. What was he saying when he was on another fox news sitcom? He said we all work for Fox news; we do or don't do what Fox wants. Huckabee is paid by

Fox news. If he does something he believes to be wrong. Judaist got 30 silver coins for selling out Jesus. Huckabee is getting paid a lot more from Fox news.

I believe almost all politicians do this in both political parties to get money for their campaign and some for personal gain.

It hurts America. Probably as much as the Fox GOP news and GOP business channels.

When I was young, very young, I read the super market tabloids. I believed what they said, much of which I found hard to believe, but I was young and believed it to be true.

Rupert Murdoch owned one of the big super market tabloids years before he started the Fox news network. Years ago, the super market tabloids were big business. The bad part is many people believed what they read.

All Television stations have entertainment news shows. Maybe not PBS, but people like to be entertained. Some do lean a little toward one political party. But if anyone who watches any fox news show and couldn't tell they were leaning; no falling over toward the GOP, doesn't have any common sense.

The GOP put our country in the hole it's in today. GOP news brainwashing the American people into thinking; G. W. Bush could do no wrong, helped.

When the GOP came into power in 1981, the rich were paying over 69% income taxes. That rate dropped to 50%. Both the 60% and 50% income tax rate was too high? I'd love to have to pay half a million dollars income tax every year. It would mean I was making over a million.

From 1951 to1963, the highest tax rate was over 90%. From 1964 to 1980, that rate was from 70% to 77%. Then, came Reaganomics (spend like there is no tomorrow) and the tax rate for the rich went down to 50%. Reagan's second year as president was the time our debt went over a trillion. Our debt was around three trillion during his last year in office. Yet during his last two years in office, he lowered taxes for the rich, first to 38% then to 28%. G.H.W. Bush brought the tax rate back up to 31%.

Now, a little history to prove what the GOP is saying may be untrue. That we can't raise taxes on the rich in the bad economic times the GOP has put us in. Clinton raised the top tax rate to 39%. During the Clinton years, the richest 1% of Americans made 47% more income after taxes. The top 95% to 99% earned 19% more after taxes. The bottom 95% only got an 8% increase after taxes but they spent that 8% which helped our economy and helped the top 5% make 19% to 47% more revenue.

Doesn't this show that a fair or flat tax would hurt the rich even more than the lower and middle class? And lower taxes for the middle and lower class create wealth for the rich so they create jobs and get richer.

Cutting government spending is necessary. Getting rid of our national debt a must. Getting rid of the Bush tax cuts for the rich is good for small business. Tax cuts for the average American is good for small business. A flat or fair tax will destroy America and anyone who is trying to brainwash you into thinking it will help America is dumber than a box of rocks. If it is your representative, vote them out. If it's someone on the media, never watch them and don't buy the product of their sponsor. This is just another attempt by the GOP to screw up America more than they already have. We can't take it anymore. Call, write, or email your representative. Tell them to save America, say no to their fair tax.

We are the most powerful nation in the world. We probably have been since 1945. We ended the war with Japan by dropping nuclear bombs on Hiroshima and Nagasaki, two cities in Japan.

Japan attacked Pearl Harbor without warning. It was an American military base. I believe dropping the bomb saved many American lives. But I think if we hit a military target, we would have gotten the same results.

Watching the history channel years ago, it showed the Chinese army making an attack on the United Nations forces, mostly American, after we had crossed the line and was moving into North Korea. It was on a holiday, I believe Easter, might have been Christmas. We were caught by surprise and many Americans were killed.

My first thought was we should have dropped the bomb on China. I didn't know at the time, but the idea was considered by America. We didn't. It might have been a good thing to do at the time. But it could have been a bad thing to do. I don't believe we should have been there.

During the cold war, we built up our nuclear weapons to the point we could destroy the world ten times over. We haven't used them in war since 1945. But we do have them. I believe this is what makes us the most powerful nation in the world.

Vietnam helped us in our war with Japan. Their politics did not matter to us at the time. We went to war with Vietnam, a country with less area than some of our states. Many years later and after having around 60,000 of our military men and women killed, we got out. We lost this war. A lot of children lost their fathers; wives lost their husbands; and parents lost their children for nothing.

If we would have won, what would we have won? We now have relations with Vietnam. Which doesn't make sense to me? Senator John McCain said he was tortured while a prisoner of war in Vietnam yet he says we should not talk to Iran, Venezuela, North Korea or even Cuba. Talk is cheap and it can't hurt. Even if there's a small chance it could help what does it hurt to try?

After the September 11th attack on America, G.W. Bush declared war on terrorism. We had to do something, and I was not for sending our military into Afghanistan. Mainly because of the history of Russia in Afghanistan, and Americas history in Vietnam. Bush administrations goal was to capture Osama Bin Laden, destroy Al-Qaeda and remove the Taliban insurgents. Osama Bin Laden is still free to hide in the hole of his choice. Al-Qaeda and the Taliban are bigger than they were on October 7, 2001 when we went in. Bush, Rove, and Rumsfeld, the GOP at its best, getting things done. Three stooges, bigots, lying to Americans. Karl Rove, now a puppet for the Fox news channel has the nerve to call Joe Biden a liar.

Afghanistan's main cash crop is the poppy, used to make opium and heroin. It would be good if we could get them a new cash crop. One that would be good for their economy. I'm against killing, but for civil rights and freedom to choose the religion of our choice. The terrorist think it's good to die as a martyr. This could be a good thing for us, the Afghanistan and the terrorist. We put a bounty on terrorist, say a thousand dollars each. It could be a new cash crop. The terrorist would like it. They would get their martyrdom and get their virgins. We could drop the bounty on Bin Laden to a thousand and get 25,000 terrorist for the price of one.

We have pictures of the terrorist training camps. We have the technology to destroy these camps wherever they are.

Let's go to the war in Iraq. Being in one war is too much.

The GOP news said Iraq was a threat to us. Later, The GOP news said they got bad intelligence, what other intelligence would you expect from the Bush administration but bad.

Fox news is saying if you disagree with Bush you're un-American. We can't wait to check facts, Bush is a leader, and he'll lead over 4,000 Americans to their deaths from behind his desk in Washington, D.C. I'll shake their hand when they come back, if they have one. War is not nice, so why did the GOP say we had to go to war in Iraq. They had W.M.D's, weapons of mass destruction, and were trying to get things to build a nuclear weapon.

As always, the Bush administration was wrong. It did surprise me. I was sure they would find weapons of mass destruction, whether Sadam had them or not.

Sadam did violate his people's civil rights. Most and probably every country violate civil rights. Some more than others. Bush and the GOP took some of ours away. They said it was for our protection. That's what

Hitler said just before he became dictator of Germany. Fox news called the civil liberties union un-American.

China violates civil rights. Remember the students protesting at Tiananmen Square in 1989? Many were killed.

Then back in 1970, May 4th, there were students protesting at Kent State. The OH National Guard killed 4 and wounded 9. Oh, that's the United States we can't go to war with them for civil rights violations. They say we won the war in Iraq, the surge worked, only over 4,000 Americans were killed and around a million Iraqis were killed. I just heard five more Americans were killed today, April 10, 2009, by a car bomb, I'm glad we won the war; it might have been ten or more killed. I'm really glad Bush and the GOP are prolife.

We didn't go to war in Iraq for the large oil reserves. But American and British oil companies got no bid contracts with Iraq. Halliburton got no bid contracts with us in Iraq. They made out.

Iraq was rushed to have elections and start their own government long before the war was over. This was good for GOP politics. Although, it caused a civil war. No, that's right; the GOP said it was just civil unrest, more people got killed. It doesn't matter what you call it. Bush said he got a democratic government started. But the new government got the right to tell us, what our military could do.

Back when Bush would go on television and talk about the war. He would come out with his sad face. I'm sorry to say we lost eight or ten of our military men or women, then get that shit eaten grin on his face and say, but were winning the war.

Bush and the GOP news would say we are taken the war to the terrorist in Iraq. This was another GOP lie. We were there and the terrorist came, and brought the war to us.

The GOP news channel is always whining about other news networks and newspapers. Well, the ones that are not owned by News Corp. anyway. GOP news used to be whining about the wall street journal, News Corp. bought it. Now, there is no whining about it, from Fox news.

Fox news talking about CNN showing a terrorist tape, a sniper about to shoot an American in Iraq. Fox news said this was hurting the recruiting of new men into our military.

I don't think it was two weeks later that E.D. Hill on the GOP and friends sitcom was telling us about finding some of our military men who were taken a few days earlier. She said they were found dead and badly beaten. Then, she said they had their penises cut off and shoved in their mouths.

If you are thinking of enlisting in the military at a time of war, I hope you would know there is a chance you may be shot. However, very few think about the chance that they could be beaten to death and have their private parts cut off and stuck in their mouths. I think this would hurt enlistment more than the thought of getting shot.

I believe the GOP could have talked Sadam into letting inspectors back into Iraq. If just talking didn't work, we could have hurt their country with covert operations, taken out all Sadam's homes to start. The GOP says their prolife. They could have saved many American and Iraqi lives with talk.

When Americans began to turn against the war in Iraq, GOP news had a lot of mothers on, saying if we got out it would mean their son or daughter would have died for nothing. Don't they think about Vietnam? 60,000 Americans died for nothing. We've had the technology for years to take a picture from a satellite that could tell if a quarter was heads up or tails. We now have the technology to hit a dime half way around the world. Why should any parent have to lose a child for nothing?

The terrorist want to die to be a martyr. If this is what they want, we should help them get the virgins they want. We offer millions for the top terrorist. Why not just offer a thousand for any terrorist. It could be a good cash crop for many of the countries that have terrorist in them. Conventional war is not working very well for us, it cost us many American military lives and many more innocent civilian lives.

Somali pirates are the same as terrorists. They could be dealt with by using technology also.

We will be getting out of Iraq soon. I'm for getting rid of 90% of our foreign military bases. But I think one place we should have a military base is right in the middle of Iraq. The government in Iraq doesn't want us to, but Cuba didn't want us in their country either. If they want us out, they can pay us back for the cost of freedom including lives.

Iran would not like us to have a military base in Iraq. The Iranian public has had hatred toward America since 1953 when America and Britain helped stop the newly forming democracy in Iran and put the Shah of Iran back in power.

For America to stop a democracy seems like something unAmerican to me. But at the time president Eisenhower was in office, he must have thought it best for America.

Shah, King or Dictator, is their a difference? If Iran's democracy had worked their might be more democracies in the area today.

Abu Ghraib is the prison in Iraq where some very terrible things were done to prisoners of war. Pictures were taken of the dreadful acts. Some of our military men including one woman were sent to prison over it. At first, some said they were following orders. One picture showed a man in a suit watching. They could have been ordered by the GOP administration to do the things they did. It should be looked into. G.W. Bush was lying when he said we had no secret prisons. We did have secret prisons that were probably doing far worst things than at the Abu Ghraib prison.

I didn't hear G.W. Bush admit he was lying about not having secret prisons in foreign countries. During a Fox news show, I heard E.D. Hill saying she was sorry when she didn't check her facts.

She said America had no secret prisons. Since Bush said we did, she apologized for saying we didn't. Then said we will see who is right. I did understand this. Did Bush come right out and say we didn't have them or just mislead people into thinking we didn't have them.

E. D. Hill wasn't to smart, but she did have great legs. I cannot believe Fox let her go.

I didn't hear CBS news say anything about her or any of the Fox news sitcoms when they mislead the American people.

Fox news was whining for weeks when Dan Rather said something about G. W. Bush's military service. Steve Doocy was a big whiner every day till Rather left CBS. Bush came from a rich family; he didn't have to go to Vietnam. What could Bush have done in the military that mattered? Did he even leave the United States while in the military?

It would be a great world without war or killing, but both have been happening since the beginning of time. Power, greed, money, religion, politics and even love are reasons man kills or goes to war.

Animals will kill for food or to protect their young. Humans have the ability to talk and reasons.

America and the Soviet Union talked. We didn't get along, but we never went to war with each other. Had we, it would have been nuclear. We probably would have destroyed the world.

Obama wants a world without nuclear weapons. It's a nice idea, but they are here to stay. Hopefully, they are never used. America has so many that we have a hard time knowing where they are at times.

Many countries want nuclear weapons. Let them have them. But if one of these countries ever uses them, that country should be destroyed with nuclear weapons that same day.

America and the Soviet Union knew there would be no winner in nuclear war.

Talking is always better than war. Conventional war is a thing of the past. It doesn't work anymore. If it did, we would have won the war in Vietnam in less than a year. We lost in Vietnam. The Soviet Union lost in Afghanistan.

We have the technology now that we don't have to send our military into countries that have terrorist who want to kill us. G. W. Bush, Dick

Cheney, Karl Rove, Rumsfeld, went into Afghanistan and Iraq. After the terrorist attacks on the world trade center on 911, it was easy to get the American people to be for the war. We had to get the terrorist. But we should have used technology. Most of these terrorist are dumber then Bush, Cheney, Rumsfeld and yes, even Rove. The terrorist groups got larger and stronger because we went in these countries. Many can't read and were easy to brainwash by Osama Bin Laden and other terrorist leaders.

We should have gone after the terrorist using technology and small covert operations. If we would have done this and gone only after terrorist and their training camps in whatever country they were in, the war on terror would be over and maybe a million peoples' lives would be saved.

We would have to let North Korea take the credit for getting the terrorist in some of the countries they are in because of world opinion.

It could save many lives, and make the terrorist happy by giving them their martyrdom. When we see tapes of the terrorist they have their faces covered. Is this because they are cowards or just plain ugly? Either way, if we kill them and give them the martyrdom they want. The virgins they get won't want anything to do with them. They will wait for a real man.

Bin Laden like Bush would be nothing. If their daddies didn't have money, nobody would have ever heard of them. Money buys power. If it's your daddy's money who bought your power, you're a low life. You would be nothing and the world would have been a better place.

War is called a necessary evil. It is evil. I don't think America has been in a war that was really necessary since World War II. I believe America should have gotten into this war years before we did. I'm not for war or killing, but if we would have gotten into World War II at the beginning, it might have saved many more lives, and the nuclear bomb may not have been developed as soon, it wouldn't have been needed.

Terrorism has been used for thousands of years. They are terrorists in every country. Fighting them with conventional warfare has mad them stronger. The GOP and Bush Administration had America brainwashed into thinking this was the way to go. Fox news channel was for it, and they would call you un-American if you were not. GOP said Clinton could have gotten Osama Bin Laden. Because of world opinion and good old politics, we didn't get him. They would have just replaced him with another nut, who would have brainwashed more radicals into becoming American haters. Sixty thousand Americans being killed in Vietnam turned Americans opinion on the war and we got out.

Terrorism works. Al Qaeda, Hamas, Hezbollah and the larger terrorist are brainwashing many Muslims into becoming radical by misleading them, taking things in the Koran out of context.

America should fight terrorism with terrorism instead of sending our military to countries fighting a conventional war.

Use the technology we have to destroy the terrorist in any country they are in. Forget world opinion; you can't please everybody. Radical terrorist would not be pleased if we went after them in their training camps. It would hurt them if a wannabe radical terrorist thought he would be killed before he even learned to do a flip off his buddy's dirty shoes, he might not want to become a radical terrorist.

It might make him think getting a bounty for taking out the radical terrorist is better than being a terrorist and letting someone collect a bounty for killing him.

America has used covert operations for years. It should be used a lot more by our military against the terrorist.

We should get our North Korean friends to do the really bad things. We will have to let them say it's not them doing it, but the world would know America is letting North Korea do things to save innocent people from being killed.

Innocent people will be killed using technology to kill terrorist, they should be warned to stay away anywhere terrorist may be. Terrorist will say we killed innocent people when we use a smart bomb on them. They will even kill innocent woman and children and say it was us. The woman in areas where terrorist are should kill them while they sleep to protect their children.

We should even put some pig's blood in the smart bombs. If any virgins are left for the martyrs, they won't want anything to do with them because they have pig's blood on them.

We should let the terrorist know our friends, the North Koreans, are using pig's blood in all their weapons used against them. Even if they are not killed, they will have the blood of a swine in their body. If they are captured, someone might even put a little of it in their food and drink. I know once it's in your body it's there forever.

When you blow yourself up all the parts that are found of you will be put in pig's blood and then you will be fed to the pigs.

If you are a terrorist, you would be better off to get out of it and just collect the bounty for killing other terrorist. You would be doing them a favor by not letting them be killed with pig's blood, and you would get a thousand dollars.

Osama Bin Laden would love you forever if you killed him and saved him from the swine blood. I have read the Koran and I know this to be true.

The Koran is not for killing innocent people. The Al Qaeda, Hezbollah, Hamas and other radical terrorist organizations are not innocent and you can get a thousand dollars for killing them.

America with the help of their secret friend, North Korea will be using more technology to fight you and will probably have the blood of a swine in all of them.

I'm against all killing; I don't even like the idea of killing the pigs just to use the blood to kill you.

We have nuts in America. I believe most of them work for News Corp. While I was writing this morning, Fox and Friends was on. Glen

Beck was a guest. Like most of the people who have shows on Fox news, this guy doesn't get it.

Beck and the others on Fox news say misleading things to brainwash the American people, like your leaders are brainwashing you to think it's alright to kill innocent people. Read your Koran, all of it, not just the parts your leaders want you to so they can mislead you.

Hear is what Beck said April 28, 2009 on a GOP news sitcom. He said he would rather have a president who is stupid meaning our former GOP president G.W. Bush than Obama, our new president, who has more intelligence than the GOP can handle. Glen Beck said mispronouncer, instead of stupid. I don't think the GOP channel is allowed to call anyone in GOP politics stupid. Like Mike Huckabee said, we work for Fox, and we do or don't do what Fox wants. All this means is they can't say what they want. There may not be any freedom of speech on the Fox news network.

Doocy said to Beck, you are all dressed up; are you going to an interview? Glen said, yes, the cartoon network. I think this would be a big step up for Glen Beck. He does remind me of Elmer Fudd. Sorry Elmer; you're smarter. Glen would be big with the six and under kids, it would be like watching themselves on television, unless they had higher than average intelligence.

Glen, you just don't get it. You and the sitcoms like yours are hurting America. You and Bill O'Reilly say you're in the middle. That's as true as Fox news saying they are fair and balanced.

You went to the tea party protest in Texas. Fox news said all they were doing was covering the story. Glen you were up on a grand stand with a country singer and talking with a sound system so all the people at the tea party could hear what you were saying to the people watching your sitcom. I never saw a real news channel just cover a story this way.

Bill O'Reilly thinks the tea parties were alright yet about a month before; he called college students who were protesting pinheads. O'Reilly said he didn't know what they were protesting, but they were pinheads.

Bill O'Reilly didn't know what they were protesting; it might have been the same thing the tea parties were protesting. So Bill must think you are pinheads for protesting. I've put down G. W. Bush and I'll put him down more. Bush said he was the decider; he made the big decisions. America was up to its waist after one term of G. W. Bush being the decider. He got a second term. That put America where we are now. Up to our neck. How many of the Bush stupid ideas came from Karl Rove?

Is getting the GOP back in power more important to Fox news than getting America back to where it was before the GOP? You tried to mislead the American people into putting the GOP back in power. They knew the GOP put our country in the crapper. You told us Rove was one of the GOP's head advisors. So, if Rove helped screw up America under the Bush administration, why would you think the American people would be stupid enough to believe any thing he said on fox news?

Any nut stupid enough to be mislead by Rove, would believe anybody. Even the nuts on Fox and Friends that said Americans all sat around the television and heard about the bombing of Pearl Harbor. I'd believer them before Rove. You probably got more people who believe what Beck says. He said, he put a lot of stuff up his nose. When he said this, I figured it must have been glue, and it killed a lot of his brain cells. Beck says he's against the GOP and the left. O'Reilly said he's in the middle. They are as far GOP as Limbaugh, Hannity and Coulter; at least these three admit their GOP all the way. If you have a show on Fox news, it's falling over GOP; they are always putting down MSNBC and CNN. Both are more fair and balanced than Fox.

Morning Joe, on MSNBC from 6 to 9 eastern time, is an entertainment news show. It has its regular hosts whom all give their views, their different views. So the difference in morning Joe and Fox and Friends which is on at the same time is that Morning Joe is fair and balanced. In addition, the females on Morning Joe don't have to show their legs to keep their jobs. The female on Joe has enough intelligence, she doesn't have to show legs.

If you watch O'Reilly, Limbaugh, Hannity or Beck, you should always watch, countdown with Keith Olbermann. He might be far left, but he'll tell you about any misinformation on any of the GOP news shows. I think Keith needs a longer show.

O'Reilly doesn't like Keith. O'Reilly doesn't like Bill Moyers, a real news journalist on P.B.C. Moyers wanted to interview O'Reilly. O'Reilly wouldn't go on the real journalists show. O'Reilly said he would let Moyers interview him at Fox news on the O'reilly show. This way O'Reilly could cut out the stuff that made him look bad. Bill Moyers is a news commentator with journalistic integrity. It would be a first for Fox news to have on a real news journalist with integrity.

O'Reilly showed clips of one of his fox boy wonders going after Moyers, paparazzi style. All it proved was that Bill Moyers is the journalist.

O'Reilly says he's a journalist he has a paper on his wall that says so. He says Beck and Limbaugh are just entertainment shows. I'd go a little further and say the Fox news network is GOP political entertainment. The bad part is people take it seriously and this can hurt our country. The GOP has hurt our country. Reagan cut taxes from 70% to 50% for five years. Before he left office, taxes for the rich we're down to 29% and our national debt hit the three trillion mark for the first time. The average American worker makes the small and big business grow. They make our economy.

Bill O'Reilly had the highest ratings for one hundred months in a row on cable news. Bill—was this Nielsen ratings that you were going to have the FCC check out because your ratings were down a short time ago?

Maybe, the FCC should check them out for the last hundred months. Countdown is more entertaining. You're getting boring.

Common sense matters that is why you should watch Glen Beck. I'll go along with this, but Fox should add, if you believe what this brain dead nut says, you know you have no common sense.

Did anybody notice how many more blacks were on Fox news when Obama was running for president and after he won the number went back down?

When there is a big event being covered, CNN gets higher ratings than Fox. I guess when it's important people don't want to hear the Fox bias.

CNN has Anderson Cooper. If all you've been watching is Fox news, you should watch CNN. It's a 24 hour news channel; it's not a political channel. They have put on some shows that wouldn't have been on when they first started, but they know getting good journalist is more important than getting good legs.

When Obama was in Iraq, he asks them why they were always watching Fox news. Look how the Iraqis have their woman dress and look how Fox has their woman dress. Fox knows sex sells, but have you noticed lately you're not getting flashed like you used to. It's been a lot more tightly legged. If you want our military men in Iraq to stay with you, tell the FCC that your freedom to show leg is important to your ratings. Put a leg flash warning on the screen so Americans at home can cover their older kid's eyes.

MSNBC had Ann Coulter working for them years ago. Was Coulter ever far left? she couldn't have been; she talks without thinking. Fox calls MSNBC a leftist channel. Fox has coulter an a lot. Fox doesn't like Keith Olbermann, he worked for Fox Sports.

Americans pay more for health care than any other country yet our life expectancy is 42nd and our infant death rate is 45th. If you only counted developed countries, America is near the bottom of the list.

Affordable healthcare is good for our country. The GOP says we cannot afford it right now because our economy and national debt are in the crapper, where the GOP put them. The GOP stopped the Clinton administration's healthcare plan. We had a good economy and our national debt was kept down, during the Clinton years.

The GOP says they are prolife. How many infants would have been saved, if they had good health care, that the GOP stopped them from getting?

How often I've heard Fox news say we will have to wait longer to see a doctor, or we will not get as good care. Who is this we? Is it the same we who will be hurt if the Bush tax cuts are stopped?

Because many Americans don't have health insurance, people who do have to pay more. If you are a small business owner, this is less money you have to help your business grow.

The pharmaceutical (drug) companies are making a lot of money selling drugs to help you feel better, lower your pain, help you live longer . . . even make your toenails look better.

In Canada, where they have a government healthcare system, these drugs cost less than in America.

Many Americans were getting their scripts from Canada. For some, it meant they could buy food or be able to pay their rent. The big drug companies didn't like this, less profit for them.

G.W. Bush went on television speaking to the American people. He said that the drugs they were getting from Canada were inferior to American drugs. They are the same drugs. Why would Bush say drugs in Canada are inferior to ours? Are big profits for the big drug companies more important to the GOP then the health of the American people?

Then maybe big profits for drug companies are why he is against embryonic stem cell research.

If they are able to cure you with stem cells, you wouldn't have to buy drugs for the rest of your life. The GOP says it's against God's law. Christ heeled the sick; he didn't give out pills or have to put a valve from a pig's heart in your heart. This is something I had to look forward to having had rheumatic fever as a child.

Embryonic stem cells are not fertilized in a woman's body. It's done in a culture dish and used for in vitro fertilization to help people have a baby who otherwise couldn't. The embryonic stem cells that aren't used are destroyed. Killing them. Isn't this more like an abortion, than using them to save a life.

The GOP and Fox news always seem to use the word abortion when talking about embryonic stem cell research. They want you to think it's a religious thing and not political.

Fox news had a Catholic Priest on their payroll. He pushed GOP politics. Ask Huckabee, a pastor turned politician, now a host on a Fox sitcom. Huckabee said we work for Fox; we do or don't do what Fox wants. Huckabee is not for abortions. I'm not for it; people who are for it have the right to be for it. It's their body.

In my younger days, I didn't like the idea that I'd need a heart valve from a pig. G.W.'s mom got one. Many Americans get transplants. Some people's religious beliefs won't allow them to get these medical things done. They have the right not to. Many were against in vitro fertilization years ago. It is the stem cells left over from the in vitro that are used for stem cell research that might save a life. Huckabee is not for embryonic stem cell research so he believes they should be destroyed (killed) and not used for research that might save the life of a child.

Is this a religious thing? Our Bible says Christ healed the sick. Or is it a political thing which will help the big drug companies keep on selling pills and making the big profits?

What do you think about someone getting the heart valve from a pig? The drug companies will sell them a pill for the rest of their life so their body won't reject it.

I love the drug companies' commercials; many Americans do. They go to the doctor and tell him what pill they want. It's a good thing now that the drug commercials have to tell you the bad affects of the pills they sell. Most spend more time talking about the bad things the pill can do then the good. Most save the one where it might even kill you for last. Even the one that gave you nice toenails might kill you.

The drug companies even put on commercials to tell you they spend millions to find new cures. Do they really want to find a cure? That would hurt profits wouldn't it?

I think they spend more on their advertising than they spend on their research. They spend a lot on lobbyists. Maybe these lobbyists got G.W. Bush to say that Canadian drugs are inferior and to be against embryonic stem cell research that might have helped his mother, better than the pig's heart valve.

Do we need lobbyist? This is the computer age.

The drug companies give money to the food and drug administration that test their drugs. I heard this on the television awhile ago. I'm not sure what show I heard it on, but I know it didn't make sense to me then. It doesn't make sense to me now. It would be like selling weapons of mass destruction to Saddam in Iraq. It's a conflict of interest.

Rush Limbaugh made fun of Michal J. Fox because he wanted embryonic stem cell research because it might help people with his disease. Rush admitted on his show about six months ago that he's addicted to pain pills. I heard about two years ago that he got arrested for buying them on the street. Rush says it's not worth talking about.

Rush mispronounces words. He stammers and stutters. You can tell he does it on purpose some of the time. I've been on Hydrocodone. It does mess up your mind and speech. I got mine form a doctor.

I started listening to Rush in the mid nineties. I liked to hear him argue with callers. He doesn't take calls from people who want to argue anymore, it's not worth listening to someone who just talks about how great he is.

It's like Hanity without Colmes . . . . not worth watching.

Rush if you had a cure and not a pill, you might be able to argue with someone who had average intelligence. Your brain would be able tell you when your losing the argument and you could hang up or go to a commercial.

Rush and Fox call government health care socialized medicine.

That nut case Beck says communism will follow all the socialism in America. How much blood would shoot out of Beck's eyes if we get rid of our military; all of it. It's a form of socialism. What is it going to do? Turn to communism? You want smaller government, less government spending, no wasteful spending, less corruption, and no socialism. Doing away with our military would cut these entirely so Beck, Rush, O'Reilly, the GOP and all of Fox must be for getting rid of our military. Sorry GOP we can't do it. We need some socialism in America to survive, just like China needs some capitalism.

If some socialized healthcare can help save the lives of American children, it's worth it. We won't turn to communism as Glen Beck would have you believe just because we keep American infants from dying in their first year of life. Beck makes enough money on Fox news that his children can go to a doctor whenever they have to.

Beck is good entertainment, but sadly some people who whatch believe what he is saying to be fact. Our infant death rate is too high now. Sitcoms, like Beck's, want to put fear into its viewers by using the words communism and socialism. Children die because they don't get healthcare.

America will not turn to communism for giving American children health care. If you want to lower America's infant death rate, call, write, or email the companies who have their commercials on these shows. Tell them you will not buy their product if they continue to support these shows.

Embryonic stem cells should not be killed if they can be use to save a life. Don't let them tell you it's against God's law, read your Bible, don't let the GOP tell you what is God's law. The GOP gets money from big drug companies, not God.

When I worked at a place that had healthcare insurance, I went to the doctor when I was sick. If I didn't have insurance, I didn't go. I probably gave whatever illness I had to many others. I heard of free clinics in big cities. I would have been happy to have one of these to be able to go to.

America's children should get the healthcare they need. They shouldn't have to put jars in stores, resturanaunts, and bars asking for money so these children can get help with healthcare they need to live. I don't care if any of the Fox news sitcom host has to wait to see a doctor. Beck's lunacy about America heading for communism if we don't stop socialized health care will cause our already high infant death rate to get higher. The funny three on Fox and Friends are for Beck; they don't care about infant deaths. The only care about ratings and the money they make misleading you with fear and the GOPs' idiotic views.

My mother has Alzheimer's disease. She needs 24 hour care. The first health care home she was in cost over five thousand dollars a month. She's in one now that cost two thousand three hundred dollars a month. Her Medicare will not pay anything toward the cost of the assisted living home because she gets around thirteen hundred in social security. If she got two hundred dollars less, she would get help. If she couldn't dress herself, she could get help. I asked if they could lower her social security so she could get help, they cannot.

Can we go to war in another country? Yes we probably can, the GOP and Fox news seems to thing we should.

Oil will be a major source of energy for years to come. After the oil crisis in 1973 was the first time the American public had real concern. They had to wait in lines to buy gas, and they had a minimum amount of gas they had to buy. I never had to wait in line, but I saw the lines on television going around the block.

Before 1973, coal and oil were our major source of energy. Nuclear power was growing fast. Then in 3/28/79 a cooling system failure at the Three Mile Island nuclear power plant caused a partial meltdown. It could have been a lot worse. No one died. There was some radioactivity released into the air and some water contamination. This stopped the building of new nuclear plants in America.

During the Carter years was the first time I ever heard of solar cells. Carter was for research in solar cells as a new source of energy. Reagan stopped Carter's government funding of solar cells. Nuclear power is much safer now. We would be using a lot less foreign oil now if we had not stopped new nuclear plant development and solar cell research. Was Reagan for big oil? They made out and our dependence on foreign oil keeps on growing. I'm sure big oil gave a lot of money to get Reagan elected, but you voted for him. Now you, your children and your grandchildren are hurting. Big oil is making big profits.

Remember when the hybrid cars come out. They were going to get 80 M.P.G. Then they came out, and they averaged about 50 M.P.G. When gas prices were going up because our oil man president was saying things on television that got the OPECT to raise the price of their oil, I bought a 91 GEO Metro. Driving normal, I get 42-43 M.P.G. If this car had electronic fuel injection or multiport fuel injection, it could get as good of gas mileage as a hybrid and cost a lot less, to buy and repair. This is 90's technology.

Fox news will tell you that if a small car has a head on crash with a big car, the small car will lose I say if a big car has a head on with a Mack truck, the big car will lose. The Mack truck with a train, the truck will lose. Don't have a head on.

Now we have many different energy sources that are being looked at because we want to be energy self-sufficient, like we wanted to in the 70s. We are using ethanol made from corn. This raised the price of corn and meat and other food prices. It would have been better to make it out of switch grass. Ethanol cuts down on M.P.G. and can hurt seals and things in cars not made to burn it.

With all the new energy sources, we should measure twice and cut once. Are they cost efficient?

For cars, I think all electric will be great. The Lithium-ion battery is a big step for the electric car. We still need better batteries and it probably won't be affordable to the average American for years.

Wind power is clean and great in the right area. Is it cost efficient? It's been used for awhile and it is growing. It will create new jobs.

Wave power, similar to wind power, only made in the ocean. Wave power would probably take more to keep going, but waves are more dependable then wind.

Hydroelectric power is probably our lowest priced power source. It's been around a long time and is clean energy. I thought it should have been used in more dams than it was.

Why not combine the wind power technology and get power from the current of rivers. Would it be that much different?

Nuclear power is much safer now, many replacing the rods with balls that cut down the chance of meltdown to next to nothing. It's green power. Yes, you would have the nuclear waste, but it could be stored on site as it is now. What is being done at our old nuclear bomb test sites? Could it be put there?

Solar power is not just solar cells. There using mirrors to direct sun light to one area to produce heat to create energy. Electric cars have been around a lot longer than many of you think. If we had a lithium ion battery fifty years ago, things would be a lot different now. All electric cars would be the best way to go if we could keep the cost of electricity to charge them down. The lithium ion battery sounds great to me, but we still need a better battery that can be charged faster and go father on a charge. Natural gas is not a green energy, but it is supposed to be more efficient and a lot cleaner than gas.

Fuel cell is too far down the road for the average American to think about. My 1991 GEO Metro gets at least 40 mpg. If they could make a car that got this good of 'gas' mileage in 1991, I find it hard to believe they can't make one now that gets 50 mpg. which is what the Prius 'gas electric' hybrid gets.

Big cars. The 1998 Buick. It was a friend's car. He had a heavy foot and got 25 mpg. This car had everything you could want on a car, yet it got a lot better gas mileage than the 7 mpg that Rush Limbaugh said he got in his Chevy. Both are made by G.M.

Rush spent about a week whining when Obama said American's could save gas by keeping their autos tuned and keeping the proper tire pressure. Rush is taking a deep breath and saying this is the same pollution put out by his gas guzzler. I think he and the fox sitcom hosts who go along with this should all get in a room with Rush and his gas guzzler and see how long it takes for them to pass out. Now that Beck is on fox news and did the deep breathing thing like Limbaugh. I don't think the fox news hosts should do it. Beck had a guy pass out on his sitcom and Beck was breathing normally. There must be way too much pollution coming out of Beck's mouth. I think Beck's mouth is hurting American a lot more than Limbaugh's 7 ½ mpg auto. If you really care about America, don't buy any product that has a commercial on Beck's sitcom or on Fox news.

Back to Rush. He said he was going to over inflate his tires because Obama said we should have proper tire inflation. I don't recommend any one over inflate their tires. But Rush if you want to, put 150 psi of air in your tires and fly down a road that needs work. Let Beck ride along with you.

America's news room is a sitcom on Fox news was talking about the new mpg ratings Obama wants. They said the Gas companies will hold back on production if Obama does this. This is why you should demand a dollar a gallon gas tax now and high taxes on the rich. It would also help create more jobs, helping our economy. If the rich want to get richer they would have to produce more, and the rich do want to be richer. So if Obama lowers your taxes; I know he cut the 10% to 5% and the 15% to 10%. Demand he lower them more so you can have more to spend helping small business grow and the rich get richer. It's called the trickle up effect.

The higher gas tax might cost you five dollars a week more to drive to work every week on the average. The last I heard the GOP and Fox news said 40% of Americans don't pay income taxes. Stop them from taking it off your payroll check so you can share the wealth and help the rich get richer. It would help our government get its debt down and become energy self sufficient.

American oil companies were capping oil wells long before many of you were born waiting for the price to go up. Yet, they want to drill more. The price is going back up again. Supply and demand and seasonal change is why the demand is higher than the supply. Are the caps rusted on the capped unused wells? Give Rush a cutting torch if he wants to keep his 7 ½ mpg Tahoe going; he'll get the caps off.

Obama wants America to adopt California's fuel emissions test. They have no state safety inspection after a car is so old it doesn't need an emissions test, but you still need to pay the same fee for a sticker that says you don't need it. If every car in America needs an emissions tests it should be done by the government and only have to be done every 3 years.

The design of new highways and roads can save energy. Our local Wal-Mart has a better entrance exit than the on-off ramp to the bypass near it. Some red lights aren't needed. My city put in stop signs to slow down speeders. Why not put in a speed bump and fine the speeders? Stopping and starting uses more energy. Many 4 way stops are not necessary. Highway building and repair is needed. If done properly, it is good for our economy and can save energy. A huge gas tax may sound bad, but it could help keep the oil companies from raising the cost of oil giving some Arabian countries less money to support terrorism and build nuclear weapons.

I've been thinking about a dollar federal gas tax and a quarter state tax since gas dropped back below two dollars a gallon. May 20 on Morning Joe, they had a guy on that said a higher gas tax is unnecessary because gas prices will eventually go back up to $4.50 a gallon as we come out of the recession. This is why we need the higher gas tax now. Not only will it help us become energy self sufficient and cut down on green house gases, but it will create jobs helping small business grow and gets our economy going faster. If price of gas goes up slowly, only big oil companies makes out.

Within a half hour, they had the head of the GOP party, not Rush, the real one, on a clip saying we should not be thinking of 1940; we should be thinking of 2040. True! But let's think about 2010 first. When Reagan became president, the rich were paying almost 70% income taxes. When he left, they were only paying 28% and our national debt went up to almost three trillion.

The GOP keeps saying that we can't raise taxes during a recession. Yet, the GOP says we should have a flat or fair tax which would raise taxes on up to 90% of Americans. You should think of waiting till 2040 before you think about voting for a GOP politician. You could afford to help small business by being able to afford repairs on your house or car, buying more things to make your life better. The GOP says small business make our economy grow. If you are the average American and can't afford to buy the service or product the small business is selling, there won't be any small business or a growing economy. The GOP is the reason we have a high national debt. Now they say we should control our spending, but not raise the taxes of the rich because our economy is bad. Our economy is bad because the GOP lowered taxes on the rich while we went to war in two countries. If the GOP would have raised taxes on the rich which is normal when a country goes to war, we wouldn't be in the economic hole we are in now.

The biggest part of our tax dollar is used for military spending. We have around a hundred and twenty of our military bases overseas. If we brought a hundred of these bases back to America, we would still be the most powerful nation in the world. It would also cost us less and be good for our economy. Our military men and women would be safer from a terrorist attack along with America itself. We could still have our war on terrorism by using technology and terrorism on them wherever they are without sending our military into their country.

We could warn them first so the innocent people would stay away from them. Put a bounty on them and put pig blood in all the weapons that we use on them. You probably think I'm being funny about the pig's blood, but it might make a lot of them think twice about being a terrorist if they know they won't get their virgins. Give the pigs something too. Feed what's left of a terrorist that blows himself up to them. Sounds nasty. But it's not as bad as terrorist killing innocent Americans and killing even more innocent Muslims including men, women and children. The Koran is not for the killing of innocent men, women or children.

Terrorist do things to cause you to fear them. The GOP wanted you to fear them. You gave up some of your rights, and gave the Bush administration more power.

Dick Cheney shot a lawyer while hunting. He was drinking before he went hunting, and the lawyer almost died. I cannot believe an average American in any state, even Texas, could have gotten away with this.

I've heard about twenty Americans were electrocuted while taking a shower in Iraq because of substandard work by Halliburton or their subcontractors. Would you want them to do any work for you? Why would our government? Hopefully, Dick will stick to fly-fishing. Nobody should be above the law.

On Memorial day, North Korea set off a nuclear bomb and fired three short range missiles and declared itself ready for battle. Let the U.N. take care of it. America should give or sell. Sell would be better; sell six nuclear missiles to South Korea. Then get our military out of

South Korea. China wouldn't like this, but we can just tell them it's all we could do since they did nothing.

Then South Korea will also be ready for battle. Israel is always ready for battle, but we should sell them as many missiles as they want. There is a lot more to destroy in Iran. If they do use them, Obama will have to go on television and condemn them for using weapons we sold them. Tell them it was not a nice thing to do, and make them promise not to do it again before we sell them more.

There are many religions, old and new, they all have basic similar and different views. Most people keep the religion they are born into. I tried to change mine over twenty years ago, but I was told I couldn't because I was divorced. Things must have changed since then. Gingrich was divorced twice and he's becoming Catholic. I'm glad I couldn't because I wanted to change for the wrong reasons.

Is a religion started from a book? Maybe, we can start a new religion; one against killing and wars and where men and woman are equal. I've checked out a lot of religions. All seem to favor man. Why is this? Aren't all countries the same? How did we go so long without giving women the right to vote? In some countries and religions, women are not much more than property. Hugo Chavez said some nasty things about Bush and the Bush administration, so did I. Fox news said to boycott CITGO gas. This wouldn't hurt Chavez. It did hurt small business in America. Chavez doesn't own the CITGO gas stations. Americans own them. Chavez gave free heating oil to Americans in need. Fox news said they shouldn't take it. If someone needed oil to keep their family warm, would News Corp. give it to them?

Fox news, we report, you decide. You have the ability to decide what is best for you.

Our economy is number one. If it was war, you would probably not have Obama as your president. He might have still won, because the longer America is at war, more Americans will be against it.

I'm not for war or killing. But if its kill or be killed, you kill. The sixth commandment doesn't count in times of war. It's in the small print. If we can't talk to the terrorist, we have to terrorize them. If we fight them with conventional war, it gives them a chance to kill more Americans which helps them recruit more terrorist. Putting a bounty on them in Afghanistan would put fear into them. They wouldn't know who might kill them. They know an American soldier would.

If we know where a terrorist training camp is, we should destroy it, no matter what country it's in with technology and covert military actions. Covert like the Unit on CBS . . . . not like Jack Bower on 24 who lets a nuclear bomb go off in L.A. and stops in a truck when he just got away from terrorist to make a cell phone call, and lets them get the truck back.

If we kill a hundred terrorist for every one innocent person they kill, I think there would be less interest in becoming a terrorist. World opinion might be against some of these things being done so we will have to make a secret deal with North Korea or Iran to do the nasty stuff for us.

The Fox news channel says we can't raise taxes in a bad economy. They tell you if you raise taxes on the rich they won't hire. Just think about this on any level . . . no matter how rich you are, you want to be richer. In 1980, the rich were paying 69% income tax; in times of war, up to 90%. They had to hire more to make more. They had tax loopholes and off shore accounts so they could keep a lot of their money. It seems like the rich need the high tax bracket as an incentive to make more money. The Bush tax cuts for the rich didn't help America. A gold commercial that's been on television for sometime says the value of the dollar is down 27% and the price of gold is up 100% since the year 20000 when Bush was elected. We went to war. Bush should have raised taxes, not lowered them. Obama should have stopped the Bush tax cuts. The rich lost money even with the GOP tax cuts because of the value of the dollar going down.

Lowering taxes on the middle class, giving those more to spend, will help the rich and small business grow. If you make a million a year or more you should pay 50% income tax until the American debt is gone and we are no longer at war. Then your taxes can be lowered to the tax rates of the Clinton years. If the wasteful spending is stopped, the taxes might be able to be lowered even more. If we give aid to another country, we should give them the product or service they need; not money.

Fox news said you are secretly paying a thousand dollars or more a year for your health care insurance because people without healthcare go to the emergency room and don't pay their bills. I believe Obama's been trying to say this for a long time now. It's one of the reasons for the health care reform. It's why your doctor has the sign on the wall saying payment expected at time of treatment.

Fox is not for health care for everyone. They had a GOPer saying if someone can't pay for a doctor they should just go to the emergency room. This is what is costing you and your employer more for health insurance.

Carlson stopped the two from talking about health care cost before they were done. Fox news had to get to what they probably thought was a more important new story and talk to people who were giving away some cats. I'd bet Gretie could have sold the cats for them. Why give them away.

Obama made his first pick for a Supreme Court Judge. The GOP takes a statement, only a small piece of a statement, and say she is a racist. This is politics at its best, misrepresent the facts. Rush Limbaugh calling someone a racist? Rush said it takes three black journalist to make one of him. He played Barack The Magic Negro song on his show before which he had a Brokeback Mountain song which had John McCain in it. Rush didn't like McCain. If you don't like what your elected representative is doing, you can write, call or email your representative and tell them. Not enough Americans do this. Politicians get money to get elected from big business and the rich. But they need your vote. Tell them what you want.

Rush gets money from the commercials that are run on his show. You can also, write, call or email these people and companies and tell them you won't buy their product if they are paying a racist.

I was for Obama because he has intelligence and said he was against the war in Iraq. He was going to stop the Bush tax cuts for the rich and create jobs. He said he would close Gitmo, a prison in Cuba. I don't see why the location of a prison matters. It would be wasteful spending to close it. World opinion was about the treatment of the prisoners and the tortured. No one should be tortured.

Obama should stop the Bush tax cuts yesterday and give more tax cuts to the average American so they can share their new wealth with the rich. The price of oil is back up. Obama wants to be reelected, tell him you want a lot higher gas tax. America will be better faster with it.

Get out of Iraq,. No one likes a foreign military in their country. They would get the terrorist out. Free trade. N.A.F.T.A. Yes, I know it was a Clinton thing. I don't' see how it can be good for the average American or America.

During the eight years Reagan was president, he lowered income taxes on the rich from almost 70% to fewer than 30%. Nobody should have to pay 70% income tax.

I'm sure many of the very rich found tax loopholes and other ways to keep most of their money.

May 30, 2009, GOP news again with the fair tax. Cavuto is asking why he should work if the government is going to take more of his money. Work? Look at Cavuto's, Limbaugh's, O'Reilly's, Hannity's and Beck's hands. They always wave them in front of you, on their sitcoms. How many of you men or women, with only a high school education like Beck, have hands that look as soft as his? I cannot believe he reads all the books and stuff he claims to. If he read a news paper, he'd get a paper cut.

The average American worker makes our economy and makes the small business grow. You spend the money you do work for that makes the rich richer. You should be able to keep more of the money you earn. If anybody, GOP or Democrat, says they want to raise your taxes and kill our economy, which is what a fair tax will do, vote them out or don't watch their show.

If some idiot tells you that America is becoming a Socialist Country, have the government makes a 90% tax bracket for them. They don't care about America they just want to make money acting like a nutcase, wanting you to drink the Jim Jones kool-aid. Fox news talking racism. LOL! Did you notice after Obama was in the running for President, the number of blacks that were on the GOP news channels? They were on every sitcom.

I don't think they thought Obama had a chance to win. I don't think there are near as many on Fox news now as before. There was Kelly Wright, who I first saw when he was their Washington news person. I thought this guy was good enough to work for a real news network. He has an hour show now on the weekend. But he's worked for Fox too long; they got him waving his hands around like Hannity and Beck, who don't have Kelly's education.

One thing Fox news got right is we can't just print more money. Yet, we are. They had it on 60 Minutes on CBS. We are at war. Look back in history, not Beck's history, real history. The rich paid up to and over 90% of income taxes in times of war. If we said we were going to have a 90% income tax on the rich before we went to Iraq, do you think we would have gone to war? I think not.

Who made out in Iraq? Bush's big oil and Cheney's Halliburton.

Who lost their lives and limbs in Iraq? The average Americans in the military and hundreds of thousands of innocent men, women and children living in Iraq.

What should we do about the nut in North Korea? Nothing. Let him blow his wad and forget about him. He wants the attention so let him co-host the Beck sitcom. I'd like to see who the bigger idiot is.

I could go on, but you know my thoughts. After September 11, my stepfather said to me that he'd been through a lot in his life. He was in World War II, but nothing scared him more than the 9/11 attacks. I replied it's the world we live in. I was planning to do some work on a car. I didn't get anything done. We talked the entire day.

I know what my stepfather felt like after 9/11. The hole America is in after the last there GOP administrations scares me.

The GOP said Obama didn't have enough experience to be president. He seems to have values. Hopefully being president doesn't take these away. Tell your elected officials what you want. But know what will be good for you, not for me or anyone else . . . make America work for you and your children.

Obama has been President for eight months now. We are still in Iraq and Afghanistan, and the Bush tax cuts are still there. The stock market is going up; it has been on the rise since the end of March.

Listen to Cavuto's statement at the end of his show on April 1st especially the end when he says April fools. Who's the fool now Neil.

Cavuto has a business show on Fox news. It seems like putting the GOP back in power is more important than our economy. F.B.N. If your cable company has it, call them and tell them to get rid of it.

I never cared what party was in power. They both got money from big business to get elected and always lied to the people who voted for them.

I guess Obama is just going to let the Bush tax cuts run out. The GOP says he is raising taxes by doing this. Bush should have stopped them when we went to war in Iraq. If we go to war in any country, we should raise taxes to pre Reagan years. I'd bet we wouldn't go to war unless it was really necessary.

Let's play what if. What if after the Soviet Union pulled out of Afghanistan, America would have helped them rebuild (we're talking about doing it now). If we did it in the 80s, isn't there a chance the world trade center might still be standing. I know there are a lot of what ifs. Things would be a lot different if we didn't' stop a newly forming democracy in Iran in the early 1950s.

The GOP was always saying they needed another Ronald Reagan. He was a nice talker. He used a lot of covert operations instead of going to war which G. W. Bush should have done. But we need another Reagan like we need another G. W. Bush. Reagan said he was prolife. While governor of California, he signed a bill that allowed two million abortions. When he took office, America's debt was 700 billion. When he left, it was 3 trillion.

Then there was the Iran contra affair. Reagan said he didn't know what his national security advisers were doing. How much of what happened during the 80s did he know? If you've read the book or watched the movie, Charlie Wilson's War, Charlie was responsible for the covert operations in Afghanistan which had a lot to do with the fall of the U.S.S.R. But GOP history gives credit to Reagan.

Reaganomics was the beginning of where we are today. It also cost G. H. W. Bush from being reelected. This was a good thing; Bill Clinton was elected president. Clinton got the Omnibus Budget Reconciliation Act of 1993 passed without any GOP votes. It was a great 8 years for America. The debt was 5 trillion when he took office and 5 trillion when he left office. It probably would have been lower but the GOP got control of the House while he was president. Under Clinton, the U.S. had a projected federal budget surplus.

Then came the G. W. Bush administration and down we go. America was attacked by terrorist under the Bush administration's watch.

I don't understand the problem making a health care plan. There are a lot of countries with health care systems that work. Pick the most cost efficient one; one that works well and copy it. Then get back to work creating jobs and getting our national debt down. We can't just keep on printing money; it makes our dollar worth less.

The GOP has been telling you for months that it is Obama's economy now. The GOP has been pushing us to where we are now for the last 29 years.

Clinton slowed things down for 8 years then G. W. stole the 2000 election and put America back on the fast track to destruction.

Glen Beck is an entertainer. There is little truth to anything he says. I believe he knows the things he's says are lies, but he's going to make 20 million or more this year. Blood never shoots out his eyes, but it did leave the bodies of a lot of Pittsburgh police officers that it was said were shot and killed by a nut that believe Beck when he said Obama was going to take away his gun.

There are a lot of nuts out there who believe what the GOP nuts say is fact. It's their opinion or view. This book is what I believe. I'm sure Bill O'Reilly will call me a pin head. I believe everyone who is on the Fox network are nuts. But many people believe anything they hear on television. They are easily misled. Beck said he cares about America. I care about America. Check out my views. Fox says we report; you decide. I believe they should say this is Fox, we mislead you . . . try to figure it out.

This book is what I believe. I'm not perfect. I was wrong once. It was about 30 years ago. GOP Damned America, God bless you, and our country.

www.ingramcontent.com/pod-product-compliance
Lightning Source LLC
Chambersburg PA
CBHW050337290526
45785CB00006B/2535